Thank You

FOR COACHING ME

Petal Publishing Co

No Part of this book may be scanned, reproduced or distributed in any printed or electronic form without the prior permission of the author or publisher.

Copyright 2020 - Petal Publishing Co

COACHES' NAME

ATHLETES NAME

SPORT

YEAR

TRAINING DAYS

TRAINING TIMES

_____

_____

_____

TRAINING LOCATION

_____

_____

TRAINING GOALS

_____

_____

_____

_____

_____

YOU ENCOURAGED ME TO ...

_____

_____

_____

_____

_____

_____

_____

_____

_____

_____

_____

Inspiration

"A good coach can can change a game.
A great coach can change a life."

John Wooden

THE LOCATIONS ON OUR JOURNEY...

_____

_____

_____

_____

_____

_____

_____

_____

_____

FUNNIEST MOMENT ...

_____

_____

_____

_____

_____

_____

_____

_____

_____

OUR GOALS ...

_____
_____
_____
_____
_____
_____
_____
_____
_____
_____
_____
_____

OUR RESULTS ...

_____

_____

_____

_____

_____

_____

_____

_____

_____

_____

_____

_____

FAVORITE MEMORY ...

_____

_____

_____

_____

_____

_____

_____

_____

_____

_____

_____

_____

_____

PHOTOS

"If your
Dreams
don't
scare you,
they are
too small"

Richard Branson

YOU INSPIRED ME TO...

OUR VICTORIES ...

I LEARNED THESE SKILLS FROM YOU ...

_____

_____

_____

_____

_____

_____

_____

_____

_____

_____

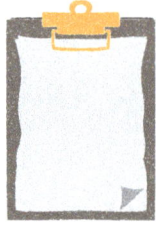

COACH, YOUR FEEDBACK MADE A DIFFERENCE TO HOW I PERFORM BECAUSE …

_____

_____

_____

_____

_____

_____

_____

_____

I LOOK FORWARD TO TRAINING BECAUSE ...

_____

_____

_____

_____

_____

_____

_____

_____

_____

_____

I WOULD TELL SOMEONE THAT WILL BE COACHED BY YOU NEXT YEAR ...

_____

_____

_____

_____

_____

_____

_____

_____

_____

_____

I APPRECIATE THE WAY YOU ...

_____

_____

_____

_____

_____

_____

_____

_____

I LEARNED THESE SKILLS FROM YOU ...

_____

_____

_____

_____

_____

_____

_____

_____

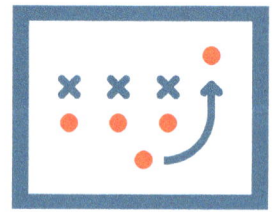

COACHES'
Keepsakes

COACHES' Keepsakes

Coaching Memories

Coaching Memories

AUTOGRAPHS

AUTOGRAPHS

www.ingramcontent.com/pod-product-compliance
Lightning Source LLC
LaVergne TN
LVHW070211080526
838202LV00063B/6589